And so...

David Glynne-Percy

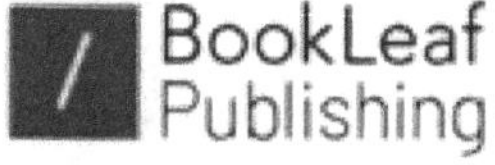
BookLeaf
Publishing

Presentation by *BookLeaf Publishing*

Web: www.bookleafpub.com

E-mail: info@bookleafpub.com

ISBN: 9789357210799

First edition 2022

DEDICATION

To Aisha and Anna for anchoring me to the
Earth.

ACKNOWLEDGEMENT

To Anne for beguiling me to enter this foray.

PREFACE

A preface to the future

Enter Me

How will you unwrap me?
Will my skin sliver easily open
When you pull?
Will you need a pointed knife?
Or clench your teeth together
Across my casing?
Perhaps you will open me
Surgically with scissors -
A neat, stretched cut
Along an exposed edge.
Or might the shell explode
From your impatient hands
Scattering my bleating innards?

And how will my contents
Sprinkle across your senses?
Do you try me on?
Do I appear to fit?
Does my shade suit?
Possibly I am to be tasted -
A potential smile taps your tongue.
Or perhaps my demi-parts assembled
Present a fixed unmoving lump.
Placed, admired, discarded, forgotten.
A complete orbit of likelihoods.

Academics' Oasis

Through coded pathways,
They gather, sheltered from the heat,
From out there - from which they report
Data- to fellow advocates,
Of how it is out there.

Each their specialty,
A niche of concern,
Extracting eternal new flavours
From familiar sucked bones
From the dust out there.

Symphonies of tensions, ruptures, dissonance
Presented in new fugues,
Denuded of metaphor
Their dictum dressage
Re-imagines the out there.

Watch how the hunched trees
Redress to sentinels
When the bleached academics leave.
And the ghost winds
Dance in from out there.

Love Song of the Sociologist

Let us navigate through congested tensions.
Allow exploration of disjunctions,
Micro-aggressions, and precariousness.
I am here to shed light upon domains
Of toxicity and their pre-requisites.
I am a sociologist.

So, let us embrace valid enquiry into
Contested disruptions,
Structural inequalities,
To reveal meanings of estrangement.
Facilitating these spaces of examination
We may shift emerging perspectives,
Temporal re-rooting,
To co-construct imagined futures.

Pattern of the Past

Recent findings suggest the earth mound was
An important focal point in local life.
"What we are potentially looking at here"
Says Professor Digby Bowles, "is
A sort of earth shrine, where people once
Congregated to celebrate birth, the transmission
Of life from one generation to the next."
Apparently the gatherings were heavily
influenced by
Female deities. But curiously the team have
unearthed relics
That indicate only one single festivity, beyond
which
The archaeological evidence runs cold.
 "It's rather odd," adds the professor, "To have
shifted
This amount earth and other debris,
Not to mention the enormous retaining wall.
It all points to a civilisation of determination and
utter boredom.
I'd like to think we've moved on since those
days."

The Garden

At weekends, the evenings
When there is light,
And the blessed holidays,
She swaps class.
Here her pupils are positioned in rows,
Chosen by colour, ordered by size
Cultivated by season.
Her pupils are mute, yet responsive,
Engrained to her touch, engaged by wisdom.
Innate triggering, predictable
Blooming under her guidance.
This is her class in which weed killer,
The cleft of her hoe, have such visible
Effect.

The Car Park

I am here again, habitually parking
Next to the blue Honda Jazz in the
Half empty school car park.
Perhaps, somewhere in the aquarium building
The blue Honda Jazz driver looks out
And spies me. "Him again," they muse, "he
With half the carpark to choose from decides to steer
into the same space each morning."
Who are you Honda driver? What halts you
From breaking out of the mould?

The Battery

The battery begins:
"Believe you can"
Strikes the large banner in Reception.
Inside the cavalcade continues:
"You are capable of more than you know"
Blasts along the first floor banister.

Pray silence to this bombardment.
We wait for the answer.
What is the school's role
Within these vacuous truisms?

The Return

This place has not waited for me.
It does not recognise my return.
It is unloving, indifferent
And into this hardness I sink,
Unfolding my crafted memories,
Which scamper across the surface,
In search of crevices on which to cling.

Windover

He captured the gaze of two summer hillsides
Unsure of which, plundering both
Of the warm evenings and the west flung sun,
That they might unfold at his command,
Alert at his heel and never expire.

The Climb

Now arise dunce and dance.
Inelegant swagger jerks the jester from side to
side
As he embraces the foot of the slope in
descending gear.
Now his tune is strained, less melodic and he
fights
To camouflage the grimace of incline, searching
Within for passages and goblets of trickery that
Keep fatigue behind an unlocked door.
And there among his armoury he seduces the
climb.
In slow progression he unravels her contours.

Wind song

Once the wind came,
Summer, long ago -
The gate post recalls -
With a caress unversed.
A gentle embrace
From a place beyond,
Utterly unknown.
A pearl of air
Drifts through the core
And glides towards
Another shore.

Habitus

You are here to learn to write like
The examiners want you to write.
And hold the brush as I do. Now
The hard bit, extend your miserable
palate of colours a thousand-fold
to portray the world in schemas of
judgement high beyond your class.
What gymnastics of being we demand in the
Name of inclusivity.

The pier

His excursion onto the pier is regular,
once a week, Sunday afternoons usually,
weather and health permitting. A steady tempo,
Sabbath outing, a full stop at the end of the
week.

Does the pier penetrate the sea?
He perambulates its protruding length,
east side out, contemplating the curve of the
shore
until he reaches the tip where the anglers wait
for orders to leave.

Or is the pier stabbing the land, an old thorn
stuck into ancient flesh?
He walks landward, promenading the west side,
the prominent
wind cuffed edifice side, where the gulls and
autumn
starlings choreograph their pulse.

His Sunday pier outing is finished. Put away in a
deep
drawer. Next week, Sunday afternoon probably,
he will return and rehearse the steps, hoping
the ballad will change the tide.

No Bradda Head

A tombstone headland gleaned
In a mirror dance, glinting
with the wind and waves
in a flash of forty years.

And there shell bound,
unfathomable and pinned,
the pitch of memory
circulates the eddies,

carved in a mausoleum,
trapped by the bandage of
time, the mind unwinds her
illusion upon the horizon.

Hommage to MacCaig

15

The windings of my small world;
These eternal journeyings will cease.
The shadows and shades, the bright spaces,
Will conclude their shifting positions,
Somersaulting over the dark overhang
That waits.

It comes to pass

From my pulpit I sermon again.
Do not squander the path to death
through the acres of
tears and laughing. There comes
a multitude of ways to display
the further self, and places
do not change only how we think
of them. Through the scurrying mist
plod on. At the end of the day,
I will hopefully find you, if
not by the easiest route.
Predestined thoroughfare?
Then bless me providence.

Lindisfarne

A two hour coach journey has delivered them
to a stunted parade of shops on a dwarf High
Street.
"Have we done it all?" she asks, entering the
café.
"Is that it?" "I thinks so," replies her companion
despondently. They approach an empty table,
two washed up walruses disenchanted by the
beach.
On their disappointing journey they have
dredged
a bottle of mead, a Celtic broach and a plastic
sword –
Viking raider no doubt, hell-bound from the
North Sea.

December 1975

Another term passes and Christmas approaches.
Still too young to panic at the rush of years.
I remember, yes I remember our brittle voices
On Winter's darkness. And yes I remember the
places
That framed our days, the boundaries and paths
That fashioned and gripped our fledgling
spheres.
And yet, and yet amid extracted distant echoes
There comes only the blur of faraway faces.

To The Beacon in pee jays

19

What you staring at?
Keep an eye on your own
basket, babe. Besides…
don't look at me like that.
I know what you're thinking-
she's still in her pjs.
Well, so what if I am?
Take care of what's in your basket,
it's contents shout a thousand tales
and I'll take care of mine.

Human

And so I plod on through the patter and clink of
days,
This unravelling of a sole life,
A dress rehearsal to the annulled performance.
And as I wander through these repeated chords,
How are these rooms furnished and does my
Evolvement across these spaces improve?
Do I exhibit an embodiment of ease
Through an osmosis of experience:
Learning to disperse clutter, the toxic,
The shadows and hollows of darkness;
The anti-matter to what matters?

Where do I go from here?

21

Let me remember tomorrow as the composer,
Inscribing the notes before they are played.
Sculptor of a dance through these awakening
Acres. The brush strokes linger towards
A future remembered light.

www.ingramcontent.com/pod-product-compliance
Lightning Source LLC
Chambersburg PA
CBHW070732160726
48003CB00006BA/2473